This book is to be returned on or before
the last date stamped below.

MANIFESTOS FOR THE 21ST CENTURY

SERIES EDITORS: URSULA OWEN AND JUDITH VIDAL-HALL

Free expression is as high on the agenda as it
has ever been. though not always for the
happiest of reasons. Here, distinguished writers
address the issue of censorship in a
complex and fragile world where people with
widely different cultural habits and beliefs are
living in close proximity, where offence is easily
taken, and where words, images and behaviour
are coming under the closest scrutiny.
These books will surprise, clarify and provoke
in equal measure.

Index on Censorship is the only international
magazine promoting and protecting free
expression. A haven for the censored and
silenced, it has built an impressive track record
since it was founded 35 years ago, publishing
some of the finest writers, sharpest analysts and
foremost thinkers in the world. In this series
with Seagull Books, the focus will be on
questions of rights, liberties, tolerance,
silencing, censorship and dissent.

HISTORY THIEVES

ZINOVY ZINIK

LONDON NEW YORK CALCUTTA

Seagull Books 2010

© Zinovy Zinik 2010

ISBN-13   978 1 9064 9 778 1

British Library Cataloguing-in-Publication Data
A catalogue record for this book is available
from the British Library

Typeset and designed by Seagull Books, Calcutta, India
Printed at Graphic Prints, Calcutta

CONTENTS

'No Eastern Jew goes to Berlin voluntarily. Who in all the world goes to Berlin voluntarily?'

Joseph Roth
The Wandering Jews (1927)

DWARF LONG NOSE

And God saw the light, that it was good: and God divided the light from the darkness.

And we can now distinguish one object from another and each object from its shadow. But how do we tell a relative from a friend, a Jew from a gentile?[1] Whatever the Bible and neuroscientists have to say about it, this momentary act of recognition—recognizing someone or being recognized by someone—comes like an unexpected

1 We are not infrequently baffled by our perception of reality. I was once sitting with friends on the terrace of a Mediterranean hotel, watching locals in a cafe across the square, who were evidently involved in an emotional conversation. 'How lively Mediterranean people are! Look how energetically they gesticulate while talking to each other,' remarked one of us. 'You're wrong,' another enlightened us, 'they're just trying to shoo away the flies.'

flash of light in the darkness and gives us the warm sense of belonging.

And the opposite is true: every instance when we feel we are being ignored, not recognized by the one whom we regard as a close friend, is the moment of the most painful rupture with humanity. It feels like waking up one morning only to discover, as Kafka's hero did, that you have turned into an insect. This is not a metamorphosis. This is a nightmare. It takes place while you are dreaming.

And, perhaps, this fear of waking up as an unrecognizable monster who has lost touch with humanity makes us look a little harder in the mirror every morning.

And a fairy tale that haunted me all through my childhood was also a story of a frightening metamorphosis in a dream. Let me tell you the outline of an old German fairy tale called *Dwarf Long Nose*, which was first read to me at bedtime by

my grandmother. It tells the story of a
beautiful boy, Jacob, who was transformed
into a hideous dwarf when he fell asleep in
the magic house of a grotesque old woman,
a repulsive witch. The boy, Jacob, who
helped his mother in the marketplace at a
vegetable stall, was sneering at the witch's
ugly wrinkly features—her long hooked
nose reaching her chin, her skinny neck
and her fingers like the tentacles of an octo-
pus with which she unceremoniously
touched and squeezed the beautifully
arranged vegetables and herbs on his
mother's stall. The witch, insulted, promised Jacob that one day he would have the
same long nose, a crooked back and no
neck at all. She bought six cabbages—they
looked like six human heads in her hands—
and demanded, as was her habit, that Jacob
help her carry the basket to her house.

And it was a long journey for Jacob
into a remote and unknown part of the city.
The old woman's house looked small and

crumbling. But when they stepped inside, Jacob saw a palace with marble walls and glass floors, encrusted with ebony and gold. The old witch cast aside her cane and glided over the glass, gracefully pulling little Jacob along. She sat him down on the sofa at a kitchen table and cooked him the most delicious soup he had ever tasted, with a magic herb in it. This made him both happy and drowsy. He fell asleep and, in his dream, the old witch took off his clothes and replaced them with animal skin, thus turning him into a squirrel.

And, from that moment on, Jacob, together with other squirrels and guinea pigs who were running up and down the stairs of the house, all in human apparel, became a slave to the old witch, cleaning her house, gathering morning dew for her drinks and dust specks off the sunbeams for her bread, and learning to cook the most exotic dishes for her venerable taste. One day, while cooking soup, he found in the larder a beautiful herb he had never seen before. He sniffed it, sneezed and woke up. The house was empty. He shut the door behind him and returned to his mother's stall at the market.

And everyone on the street was laughing at him, calling him names. His mother didn't recognize him; she chased him away, shouting that he was abusing the memory of her beloved son who, she said, had disappeared seven years ago! Jacob went home to see his father. But his father, a shoemaker, didn't recognize him either and suggested he make him a leather case so he wouldn't hurt his long nose. Jacob looked in the mirror in a barber's shop and saw a hideous dwarf with the hooked nose reaching his chin, a hump on his back and no neck at all—just as the old witch had promised. The 70 minutes of Jacob's dream had been seven years in the outside world and nobody, not even his parents, could recognize in the dwarf the beautiful boy he had once been.

And the story has a happy ending. Jacob eventually finds the same herb that he had seen in his dream and that had woken him up. He sniffs the herb, sneezes and returns to his original self. This second awakening—this time after the life of trials and tribulations of being an ugly outcast— is like a second coming. The tale is riddled with allusions to and parodies of some of the biblical motifs and images of which I wasn't aware when I first heard it from my grandmother. Neither was I conscious of the nationality of Jacob. 'In one of Germany's big cities,' reads the beginning of this tale by a precocious German writer, Wilhelm Hauff (1802–27). The fact that Jacob's story happened in a foreign land added an additional spookiness to it. But the geographical borders of my childhood imagination were limited by those of my Soviet motherland. Germany was a land of fairy tales.[2]

And the recurrent images of alienation in this fairy tale are now associated in my

Dwarf Long Nose. Illustration by Fritz Bergen.

Wilhelm Hauff (1802–27).

2 The story of Dwarf Long Nose was therefore my first link to Germany. My first visit to Berlin was a kind of return to a country of my childhood: Soviet boys playing war games apprehend the enemy with the German shout *'Khande khokh!'* But it took me quite a long time to come to Berlin to discover all this—as long, perhaps, as it took post-war Germany to come to terms with its own past after the nightmare of Nazism, which, in seven years, turned an enlightened *mädchen* into un ugly anti-Semitic witch.

mind with voluntary or enforced exile: the loss of one's home, the sojourn in a strange land and the shock of homecoming when you're no longer recognized by your friends and relatives, and the dream-like existence in which you lose the sense of time and place until you wake up one day to realize that you have become irredeemably old and ugly.

And the story I'm going to tell you in this book is also inspired by a dream. When we hear a man declare that he has had a dream, we usually expect it to be a vision of the future—an ideal future for himself, his home, his country. Having been born and grown up in a country that was designed as a utopian society but turned into a tangible hell—the USSR—I'm instinctively averse to dreaming the future. My dream was about an ideal home too. But this ideal home turned out to be located not in the future. My dream foretold my past. The

dreamy image was materialized a year ago
in a foreign city, hardly familiar to me.
An encounter, preceded by that dream, re-
vealed a link, a bridge between my awkward
émigré present and my family past that I
was not aware of. This discovery has
changed me—not beyond recognition, I
hope, but irreversibly.

BY THE RIVERS OF BABYLON

And the story of Dwarf Long Nose has a
definite moral streak—the witch makes a
beautiful boy feel with his own skin what it
means to be perceived as an ugly outcast or
an alien and to be jeered at by the mob. I
was definitely disturbed both by the image
of that old woman with a long hooked nose
who was publicly abused by a little boy, and
also by the retribution for these acts of
abuse: being shunned and not recognized
by your own parents, despite the desperate
shouts, 'It's me, mummy, it's me!' And that

long nose—the whole sense of monstrous deformity—was definitely familiar to me when I looked around at my Jewish relatives, even at the face of my grandmother in her later years. But all these moral conclusions and associations with the Bible, exile and Jewishness are made by me, retrospectively, from the point of view of someone who is no longer a Soviet child.

And unfortunately (or fortunately), I was born into a family that had been assimilated for at least three generations. My father was a communist and the only notion of God I ever came across in my youth, besides the theology of Marxism–Leninism, was drawn from ancient Greek mythology which, in an ironical twist of the country's educational system, was much encouraged in Soviet schools. But we never learned about Moses or Jesus.[3] I never heard a word of Yiddish or Hebrew spoken at home, never went to synagogue and never saw the Bible.[4] None of my close relatives perished

Zinik with his grandmother, c.1950.

3 Later, I found out that Stalin was very fond of ancient Greece. His favourite bedtime reading was a book called *What Ancient Greeks Thought of Their Gods and Heroes*.

4 When I eventually saw the full Jewish edition of the Bible, I was first and foremost struck by the layout of its pages. Each passage of the biblical narrative occupied a smaller space on the page because it was surrounded by numerous commentaries. According to the Jewish tradition, the meaning of the biblical text is inseparable from its commentaries. I have tried to adopt a similar style in this book: here, the commentaries appear alongside the main body of the text. You can also read these commentaries as

in the Holocaust or in the Gulag. My Jewish
origin was stated in my Soviet internal passport—a kind of ID card in Russia—but I
was evidently too much of a conformist and,
therefore, too reluctant to dig deep enough
in search of my Jewish roots for fear of
discovering that I was not like everyone
else. Apart from an occasional exchange of
nastiness in the playground—common
among adolescent boys in every country—
I had never heard an anti-Semitic remark
directed at me personally, nor had I ever in
my life or my career suffered from an anti-
Semitic deed or gesture on the part of any
organization or institution in the USSR.[5]

And I didn't run away from the Cossack's
sabre, nor from the tsar's secret police. In
1975, when I decided to apply for an exit
visa to immigrate to Israel, the officials were
trying—in many cases quite sincerely—to
dissuade applicants from leaving Mother
Russia. Although voluntary exile from the
Soviet land (without the right to return)

a separate text or ignore them altogether, as Christians did when they plagiarized the Old Testament.

A page from the Talmud.

5 This is true only in a limited sense. Throughout my life in the USSR I was reluctant to reveal my ethnic origin to strangers. As for my double-barrelled surname (Gluzberg-Zinik, as it is printed in my British passport), I was always more inclined to be called Zinik than Gluzberg, which sounded far too German-Jewish for the Slavic ear. Zinik was also my nickname since childhood and was passed on

Zinik (left) in Moscow, c.1960.

meant complete separation from friends and family, from my native city and language and everything that life was made up of, I moved out with my entire past in my mind and my personal archives in my suitcase. I left my Soviet *Vaterland* with no regrets and no serious trauma or bitterness. The Moscow of that era was, for me, the most entertaining prison in the world, but I also wanted to see what was happening outside the prison gates.[6] The only way available to me, being of no propaganda value to the Soviet authorities, was to emigrate. Since by word of mouth from relatives to friends until it finally crept into my passport as my second name. This fear of exposing my origins shows how unwelcome the outside world felt to me, a Jew. And I had always been aware of the quota system for Jews at the University of Moscow in my time. I pretended that this applied to everyone of any origin in the USSR's ethnic melting pot. In the late-1960s, as a minor samizdat author, I started to use Zinik as a literary pseudonym. Since then, it has become a token symbol of my second nature. Literary activity was then—and still partly is—regarded as a sacred and mysterious occupation in Russia. It is also identical in my mind with my Russian youth, so that, with my emigration from Russia in 1975, these two names began to represent two different ages of mine, two aspects of time in a life which existed simultaneously—one of the natural ageing process, and the other, connected with the name Zinik, of fictional age or my literary alter ego. As all my published novels have been written since my departure from Russia, this second age of mine is associated with my émigré persona. This persona is one of eternal youth because the self-perception of an émigré is forever frozen in time, tied up with the moment of fateful departure.

6 Unless you were in open confrontation with the authorities, you could, in a freakish way, enjoy the life of the big and boisterous city that was Moscow. With plenty of state money still around, the arts scene allowed quite a few diversions from the Party's general line. My older peers and then, I've written a few novels arguing quite successfully why people like me succumbed to an urge as mad as to leave their own country for good. Now, I can only say that the urge to get out was stronger than my attachment to my native land. I wanted to emigrate so that I could experience the feeling of being an anonymous foreigner.[7]

And this, the most important step of my life—emigration—turned out to be an act of fabrication of my past, or so it seemed at the time.[8] The USSR, under pressure from the US and in exchange for trade agreements with the West, had decided to improve its human rights record by relaxing restrictions on travelling abroad for ordinary citizens. Members of a family, divided by the Iron Curtain after the war, were granted the right to be reunited. You were allowed to emigrate from the USSR, ostensibly to join your relatives abroad. So, everyone who wanted to leave had to trace an mentors, who used to frequent the Café Artistique oppo-site the Moscow Arts Theatre, would talk about Paris and London without ever having been there and quote James Joyce and Aldous Huxley as if they were next-door neigh-bours. It was a bizarre version of cafe society in a prison-like city. Life was only enhanced by the proverbial Russian warmth of closely knitted relationships within a tight clan of friends, the sense of chosenness about belonging to the spectacular Russian spiritual history and the prominent place the writer occupied in the Russian psyche. All this made the old fear—of finding oneself outside the proxim-ity of Russia—more acute than ever, and the decision to emigrate more precarious.

7 Even today, 35 years after my departure, at every social gathering, I always wait for the inevitable clichéd question: when, why and how did I leave Russia, and do I intend to go back? There is a subconscious tendency in people to define strangers by their ethnic origin, and strangers in turn resent this attitude with a passion similar to that of children who resent remarks about their resemblance to their parents. In this war of stereotypes, I am on the side of the children: although I know now that it is impos-sible to rid ourselves of the past, it is exactly the attempt to do so that constitutes our sense of freedom and moulds our personality.

8 Jewish history is always somebody else's history. Those who are disillusioned with their own present are in search

uncle or aunt—real or semi-invented—
beyond the Soviet borders. For a citizen of
Jewish origin, this was not that difficult a
task, thanks to the disparate geographical
character of the Jewish diaspora. In the
cosmopolitan Moscow of the 1970s, people
joked that Jewishness was not an ethnic cat-
egory but had become a means of trans-
portation. The snag was that once the exit
visa was granted, your Soviet citizenship was
annulled and you couldn't return to the
USSR. Dissidents of any kind would leave
their mothers and fathers, spouses and children, oxen and donkeys on the rivers of the
Soviet Babylon in order to embrace Western
freedom, personified in a fictitious cousin.

And a relative abroad, therefore, had to
be invented. Whatever I had heard accidentally about my family history was frag-
mented, anecdotal and highly unreliable.
There was no proper family archive to be
looked into. All the documents were strewn

of a fictional past that explains and vindicates their current troubles. We are familiar with people who steal someone else's past, his or her life story, by falsifying their passports or forging birth certificates. Commonly known as swindlers and crooks, they commit these acts of fraud either to evade justice or to get rich by illegal means. It seems that Jews do it for no pecuniary purpose. They do it because they sincerely believe in someone else's past as if it were their own, even though stepping into someone else's shoes is frequently wrought with undesirable consequences. Their quest is the search for a new sense of belonging. The aims are different, but the methods—a deception or self-delusion—are familiar to any outlaw. This, perhaps, is why Jews—history thieves—attract those who are fascinated by any kind of criminality.

around in a disorderly fashion among my cousins and uncles, some of whom I had heard about but never met. Some of the relatives might also have immigrated to the West after the Bolshevik Revolution.[9]

And, as it turned out, the authorities didn't care much about the veracity of my personal story. For them, I was merely one of the nuts and bolts in the machine of trade agreements and peace treaties with the West in which Jews and human rights were hard currency. My first forgery was successful. A Soviet official, a sturdy woman, took my red Soviet passport from me, cut it into pieces and dropped it into a dustbin. In its place she shoved a pink piece of paper into my hands—my one-way ticket to the West, an exit visa to Israel via Vienna.

AMONG THE BELIEVERS

And my miniature exodus out of Russia was rapid and easy. Having landed in Vienna—

Zinik (extreme right) at his farewell party in Moscow, 1975.

9 Our young Soviet pioneer minds remained free of any link to the pre-Revolutionary past. I lived inside a time capsule—in a circle of close friends, partners and lovers (ethnically a motley crew)—in which the network of almost tribal relationships created a separate universe. It was not an underground or dissident circle of activists. It was a parallel world that was included in the Soviet universe but refused to be a part of it. And, since I had become averse to this particular geography of belonging, I

a transit point—I joined a line of refugees
waiting to be allocated to different Western
countries, according to the respective immi-
gration quotas. I could have remained in
Europe if I had claimed political asylum.
But right from the beginning of my life outside the USSR, I had decided that I would
never settle down in any country unless I
was properly invited there. Henceforth, I
proceeded on my way to Israel, the country
that had issued the initial invitation.

And the only moment of doubt about
my final destination came when, along with
a group of other immigrants, I was taken in
the middle of the night from a Viennese
refugee centre to the airport to be put on an
El Al flight to Israel. The minibus dropped
us with our guide on the border of the air-
field in front of a mesh wire fence with a
watchtower. The steel gates opened and I
saw the path brightly lit up by the blinding
floodlights and lined with Austrian police,

had no choice but to look for someone else's past. At such instances, we usually turn to our ancestors—some of my friends adopted someone else's Russian pre-Revolutionary past as their own and joined the Russian Orthodox Church—but most Jews do not know their family history beyond their great-grandfather's generation. Beyond this point in the family tree, there grows the branch of uncertainty upon which Adam and Eve sat in Paradise.

Zinik with his daughter in Jerusalem, 1980.

each with an Alsatian on a lead. The collective Jewish memory, so far successfully suppressed in my mind, was stirred disturbingly up by their brief commands—'Hurry! *Schnell*!'—as we were rushed along the line towards the aircraft which was waiting for us at a distance, luminescent in the darkness before the dawn like some alien ship. At this moment, the thought quickly crossed my mind that I might have chosen the wrong way of being reunited with my fictitious uncle. Inside the aircraft, however, we were greeted by a very sexy Israeli stewardess who apologized for the inconvenience caused by the unusual way of boarding the plane—there had been a terrorist attack in Vienna around that time and the Austrian police had taken every possible precaution and security measure while transporting the Jewish immigrants to the airport.

And the first thing I saw the morning after my arrival in Jerusalem was a mosque on the top of a hill, like a snapshot, framed

by the window of my friend's house where
I had stayed that night. I accepted the
sight of this mosque as part of my new
world, my new life, my newly found
freedom. Just as I accepted Hasidic
Jews in their bizarre garb, who fought
each other over the different ways of
tying their laces or brandishing their
side locks as these minute details might
seriously delay the coming of the Messiah,
and who, at the same time, denied the
state of Israel the right to exist because the
Messiah hadn't come yet. I accepted an
Arab in his long white shirt, like that of a
mediaeval psychiatric patient, who was let-
ting his sheep graze on the manicured
lawn of a luxurious hotel in the heart of
Jerusalem. And a Moroccan Jew who swept
streets and cooked strange Arab dishes in a
Jewish market. I also accepted my former
compatriots, Jews from Russia who were
enthusiastically building yet another of
those many walls in Israel to divide two

people living on the same territory.[10]
I hadn't yet realized then that somebody's
invented past could clash with someone
else's present. I accepted many more
things that I shouldn't have.

And what I couldn't understand at all
was what I, a Soviet boy, had to do with all
of this? The same question, as far as I
know, was asked by Viennese Jews (don't
forget—I arrived in Israel via Vienna)
when they, the crème de la crème of European sophistication, had heard Theodor
Herzl urging them to settle in Palestine.[11]
I had nothing to do with the past that had
been imposed on me in Israel, where, by
the way, I was addressed, in a casual manner, as a 'Russian' in reference to the country of my ancestors. This past was invented
for me by the founders of the state of Israel
who, in constant search for new recruits,
had transformed the Jewish longing for
home into a political dogma, wrapped in

10 Some of them, no doubt, came from Russia as Subbotniks (literally, Sabbatarians), one of the Judaizing sects that initially emerged in the fifteenth century in the Russian town of Novgorod under the influence of a group of sectarians from neighbouring Lithuania. Like Muslims before them, the Subbotniks didn't recognize the divinity of Jesus Christ and negated the doctrine of the Holy Trinity. They also denied the divinity and authority of the existing Church. They conducted their religious life by following the Old Testament laws, prohibitions and rituals. Other sects of the Judaizers went even further and proclaimed themselves to be Jews in every possible sense of the word. They circumcised their children, kept strict kosher laws and observed Sabbath on Saturday instead of Sunday. Not without a considerable influence even on the tsars in their early years, they were eventually chased out by Russian Orthodoxy and persecuted by the government, especially in Stalinist USSR. They migrated to the remote parts of the country (some of them are still to be found in Siberia) and resisted all changes. A considerable number of them (according to some estimates there were 2.5 million Subbotniks and other Judaizing sectarians in twentieth-century Russia) immigrated to Israel in the 1970s and were accepted there by the Rabbinical authorities as Jews. They were put up in high-rise apartment blocks built by the state around Jerusalem and around the remaining Arab villages such as Neveh Yaakov, where I saw them wearing the Siberian peasant's garb against the backdrop of the Judean the shiny cellophane of biblical vocabulary.[12] There were ardent Stalinists among the Zionists too, some of whom are still alive.[13] But, for some inexplicable reason, I fell in love with the country, despite—or perhaps because of—these contradictory tendencies.

And I learned Hebrew with miraculous speed. I had the good fortune to be introduced to the great biblical scholar Nehama Leibowitz, with whom I began to study the Bible.[14] In her commentaries, she attacked the main body of the text from different angles, sometimes from contradictory points of view, in order to divest it of its obscure meaning, expose its varied facets and then to dress it up again with new significance, changing our understanding of it beyond recognition.

And it was Leibowitz who told me why certain Jewish sects in Jerusalem still dressed in such an eccentric manner, as if hills. (They are more accepted in Israel than the Black Hebrews from New York.)

11 This is exactly the question that the insolent son from the Talmudic tale asks his father when the festive rituals of Passover, celebrating the Exodus from Egypt, are being performed. This cheeky young Jew is exposed as a duty dodger, a denier of Jewish suffering. But to be accused of denying your past you have to have a past recognized as your own.

12 The idea of reclaiming an ancient language and territory from the past as the foundation for a modern nation-state is not original and has been used at other instances in world history: the creation of the modern state of Greece is one example. Ideology based on the myths of the past is more durable because, unlike utopian promises of a radiant future, its veracity will not be tested as time goes by. It will never be exposed as a false prophecy, and there is no need to adjust it. That is why fascism, in its many modern manifestations, is still alive and kicking, while communism is dead and buried.

13 We shouldn't forget that it was Stalin's vote at the 1948 session of the UN that was crucial for the establishment of the state of Israel as we know it. My theory is that he voted that way because he regarded Israel as the only country he could have escaped to if in need of political asylum. (His background as a student at a religious academy also played its role in his fondness for Palestine.) Stalin's notorious anti-Semitic campaign 'Fight against Cosmopolitanism'

transported into our time from another
age. They all came from a region in Poland
where one of the chief rabbis sent his emis-
saries to Paris every year so that his flock
could keep up with the current French
fashion. This habit had lasted until the
rabbi's death sometime in the mid-seven-
teenth century. According to the Talmudic
interpretation of the Law, a Jew should follow his father's way of life, death and dress
strictly. Therefore, the Parisian fashion of
black hats trimmed with fur, silky caftans
and white stockings, which had been all the
rage a few centuries ago, had, with some
modifications between the different sects,
been preserved unchanged by subsequent
generations up to now.[15] To put it in a less
Talmudic manner, these Jews couldn't forget the way they had lived in Poland before
they were exiled to Palestine. In the same
way, Odessan Jews in Brighton Beach, New
York, couldn't forget their Soviet Russian
past either, which, in this case, was reduced

(1948–53) was not necessarily in contradiction with his pro-Zionist voting at the UN: the worst enemies of Zionism are cosmopolitan Jews. It is the appropriation of individual suffering by the collective will that turns a noble longing for nationhood into hideous state propaganda. It took the ideological revolution of the 1960s in Israel and the collapse of the USSR in the 1990s to expose the falsity of this Soviet version of the dream of Zion.

14 I was introduced to Nehama Leibowitz by Leonid Ioffe, a poet and close friend from Moscow, who, at a certain stage in his life in the 1970s, had decided to eradicate his Russian spiritual roots and transplant himself on to parched Israeli soil. Paradoxically, this had not affected his loyalty to Russian poetry, as if it were safely detached from his ancestral Jewish legacy. I was so fascinated by this evident clash of loyalties that it swayed my decision to join him in Palestine in order to fully understand this conundrum.

15 One of the first recorded and best remembered instances of assumed past or stolen identity—when someone else's clothing is used deceptively as a literal cover-up—is the biblical story of Jacob, who was prompted by his mother to steal his father Isaac's blessing and the first-born's rights from his brother Esau by dressing up in Esau's furs. Conversely, Adam and Eve were naked in the Garden of Eden and were not aware of it because they had nothing to hide: they had no past to tell of. According to Leibovitch's commentary, they saw that they were naked to the basics that their stomachs felt nostalgic about. On the distant shores of the river Hudson, they recreated the staple Slavic diet they had been used to in their previous lives—pickled cucumbers and salted herring, bagels, rye bread and boiled potatoes.[16] This ordinary Russian food, smuggled from Russia by the waves of Jewish immigrants into the West, has become known in the US and Europe as Jewish. It is one of many instances when, just like with Hasidic fashion, the plagiarized tradition is taken for the original. In fact, this very Slavic salted herring was imported to Russia from the Netherlands by Peter the Great. Russians have always looked for their identity outside the confines of their national history. They invited the Vikings to conduct their state affairs for them and turned to the Greeks of Byzantium for their religion.[17]

And the moment you change your life by adopting some 'new' past, the 'old' only after having eaten an apple: not because they were blind before but because, afterwards, they were left without any laws to be obedient to. They were 'naked' before the Law since they had broken the only one they had: that they should not eat from the apple tree.

16 'We remember the fish, which we did eat in Egypt freely; the cucumbers, and the melons, and the leeks, and the onions; and the garlick./But now our soul is dried away: there is nothing at all, beside this manna, before our eyes' [Numbers 11:5–6]. It was for this nostalgic lament that the Jews were condemned by the almighty to wander in the desert for the next 40 years. This lament for the past lost in Egypt is almost identical to the Russian émigrés' complaint that German rye bread is too sticky while the Polish one is too puffy and *they* pickle cucumbers in vinegar and not in brine as they should. Perhaps the Jews sensed the loss of their immediate past lives in the countries from which they were expelled much more acutely than the destruction of the Temple in Jerusalem. At least, that was Gerhard Scholem's opinion when he described the sense of catastrophic loss that the Jews had felt when exiled from mediaeval Spain. Perhaps the Jews sat and wept by the rivers of Babylon because they knew that one day they would be told by the Persian king to go back to Jerusalem.

17 The parallel example of lost originality is the world status of the art of socialist realism. It is now regarded as solely a Soviet invention, the unique visual feature of Stalinism.

Zinik in front of the Victoria Memorial, London.

But look at the Victoria Memorial in front of Buckingham Palace [above]. The Queen sits on her marble throne (2,300 tons of white marble was used to create the monument) and two of the sculptures surrounding her are facing the Palace. One of them is a woman wielding the sickle, another a man with a gigantic hammer. It was completed in 1911 by Sir Thomas Brock and could not possibly have been influenced by the identical sculptural monstrosity of the peasant woman and the worker (with a sickle and a hammer, respectively) in front of Stalin's 'Exhibition of National Economic Achievements' [p. 37]. The style of socialist realism was created outside Russia, its proletarian motifs

*Statue by Vera Mukhina in front of the entrance to the VDNKh,
the Exhibition of National Economic Achievements, Moscow.*

Le Monument au Travail, Brussels.

were developed by different European schools—the most prominent one was the artistic section of Brussels' House of People (Maison du Peuple) [above] founded in the nineteenth century by Constantin Meunier (1831–1905)—and, throughout the twentieth century, existed simultaneously with its Stalinist manifestations in the US. The mausoleum in Moscow's Red Square is another striking example of the original lost in translation. It is regarded as a uniquely Soviet symbol of the Russian Revolution. It fact, it looks like a Babylonian ziggurat or, rather, an Egyptian pyramid. It was designed at the same time as the discovery of Tutankhamen's tomb by Howard Carter in 1922. The discovery received worldwide press coverage and sparked renewed public interest in, and fashion inspired by, ancient Egypt. The link to the Egyptian past is even more symbolic because of Freud's hypothesis that Moses was an Egyptian in Tutankhamen's time who converted the Hebrews of Egypt to monotheism—the religion of the pharaoh's dissident uncle. The image of Lenin as a Bolshevik Moses, entombed in the mausoleum, is not far-fetched, given the prophet-like iconography of the father of the Russian Revolution—which was turned into this Revolution's mummy [below].

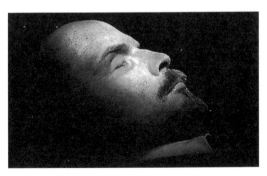

Lenin's mummy at Red Square, Moscow.

abandoned present acquires a nostalgic
patina of a complete and profound past
experience. There was the biblical sense of
guilt associated with departure from the
Promised Land; the same sense of guilt was
induced by the Party propagandists of the
utopian Soviet state separated from the rest
of Europe by the self-erected Iron Curtain.
The same curtain separates the émigré
world from the motherland. The sense of
time and space of the ghost-like existence
become distorted as in a Gothic novel. Any
fatal departure from the familiar territory
for a distant shore creates the illusion in
which your past life becomes something
like the outlines of the plot of a ready-
made novel—and emigration itself becomes a literary device. This novelistic
integrity of the 'lived-for-real' past clashes
with the utopian past manufactured for you
as the ideology of your new life, of your
new present.[18]

18 It seems that two motifs prevail in Judaism: those of the Exodus from Egypt and the return to Jerusalem. The Exodus is a liberation from slavery. The return to Jerusalem is linked to the anticipation of the Messiah. But every Jewish exodus is tied in with an upsurge of nostalgia for the land left behind, while every attempt at returning to Jerusalem is wrought with tragedy and bloodshed and, hence, constantly postponed.

And I attempted to depict this clash of contradictory attitudes to the past in my first short novel *The Notification* (1976), published in Russian in an Israeli émigré periodical. The hero of this novel, a new immigrant in Jerusalem, whose vivid memory of his Moscow past and the sense of guilt for betraying those who were left behind (including his wife who died on the night of his departure to Israel) has entrapped his mind in the life he abandoned. He lives in his memories as if in a dream, his self-perception forever frozen in time, tied up with the moment of his fateful departure. When he finally wakes up, he realizes that many years have passed and that he has become old and ugly.

And this is, of course, the plot of *Dwarf Long Nose*, my childhood fairy tale. Instead of an old witch and her dream house where Jacob, in the company of squirrels and guinea pigs, learned to cook exotic dishes, I had my hero employed in his dream by

Émigré magazine The Time and Us *in which Zinik's novel* The Notification *was first published in 1976.*

a voluptuous woman who ran a bizarre
Zionist agency in Jerusalem. Using his gift
of imitating other people's handwriting, the
hero falsifies letters from Russian immigrants in Israel, now dead, to their spouses
in Russia to convince them that their hus-
bands are still alive and encourage them to
immigrate to Israel. My hero finally man-
ages to break free from this nightmare only
to discover that, after many years, he has
been changed beyond recognition—he is no
one's friend or relative any longer.[19]

And, *The Notification* provoked an
avalanche of critical abuse and condemna-
tion. I was accused of anti-Zionism and
pornography (I denied the first charge). As
a result of this turmoil in the émigré press,
I got a good publisher in Paris. It was while
I was in Paris that the BBC invited me to
come to London. Ten years later, I became
a British citizen.

19 My decision to use the plot of *Dwarf Long Nose* was also prompted by the fact that Wilhelm Hauff's fairy tale is full of parodies of biblical imagery. The hero is not accidentally called Jacob. The witch's servants, squirrels and guinea pigs, who run up and down the stairs, are like angels on Jacob's ladder in the Bible. (The biblical place where Jacob had a dream about angels on the ladder to heaven is called Bet-El. In modern Israel, it is now the location of a training camp for new army recruits. Instead of angels from heaven, you can see Israeli marines climbing up and down the ropes that hang from helicopters.) The witch turns Jacob into a squirrel by taking off his clothes and replacing them with a fur skin, which is exactly what the biblical Jacob's mother does when she dresses up Jacob to be mistaken for Esau by the blind Isaac. The story is also a case of true identity being perceived as a fabricated one. When Jacob is not recognized at the market by his mother, he goes to his father, who tells him—a stranger and a dwarf—the story of his son's disappearance. Having realized what had happened to him, Jacob goes back to his mother and tells her how he had disappeared seven years earlier, being abducted by a witch and turned into a dwarf. Jacob's mother, half-convinced, takes the dwarf back home to consult her husband, only to witness how Jacob's father heaps abuse on the dwarf and accuses him of plagiarism—for stealing his son's story which he had told the dwarf only a short while ago.

AN EX-ISLE'S DREAM

And I found myself in a strange civilization
of left-hand traffic, three-thronged plugs
and no central heating.[20] I woke up every
morning to the cry of seagulls. I was on an
island and, like Robinson Crusoe, was trying
to recreate a semblance of home out of the
shipwreck of my past voyages.[21] Feeling
slightly out of place again, I began to dream
a serial dream in weekly instalments which
lasted for many years. I know that nothing is
more boring than somebody else's dreams,
with their idiosyncrasies and illogicality,
which fascinate only the dreamer himself
(and his psychoanalyst). But what I'm de-
scribing here is not a dream but, rather, the
dream-like image of a house. The house was
evidently my family home, which, in my
dream, I had once lost but then regained.

And it was an old-fashioned house, with
a comfortable familiar feeling about it.
There were parquet floors, high ceilings,
wainscot panels and pieces of old furniture.
Some rooms, however, had to be reclaimed

20 Driving on the left was linked in my mind to the Hebrew way of writing from right to left. I also detected the
influence of the Judaic kosher laws in the strictness with
which hot and cold water taps were separated in British
houses. The idea would please the British Israelites, a
movement that has tried to prove the Semitic origin of the
English race ever since the seventeenth century. Its most hi-
larious tool of research was philology. In his book *The Lost
Tribes of Israel: The History of a Myth* (London: Phoenix,
2002), Tudor Parfitt quotes *The Pall Mall Gazette* of 3 April
1894, which,

> . . . announced, numbingly, that the proof the
> English were descended from the Lost Tribes
> was that *Saxon* is clearly a corruption of *Isaac's
> son*. Some oft-repeated Hebrew proofs are that
> the Hebrew *brit* meaning covenant and *ish*
> meaning man are the base of the word *British*
> (men of the covenant); the word *Britannia* is de-
> rived from *brit* and *onia* meaning ship and thus
> Britannia means ship of the covenant (and of
> course Britannia rules the waves) (p. 61).

21 An enthusiastic newcomer, I had to adapt myself to the
native habits and, yet again, change my style of dress,
manner of speaking and food preferences. This mimicry of
outward behaviour eventually affects our mode of thinking
too; not vice versa. By the way, Jacob's transformation into
Esau in the eyes of the blind Isaac consists of four stages:
Jacob puts on Esau's 'raiment'; he then places 'the skins
of the kids of the goats' [Genesis 27:16] on his hands in

from neighbours with whom we had to share the landing: they were squatters but we couldn't get rid of them because they had been residents of the place for too long, from even before we had arrived to repossess our ancestral property.[22] In order to get to some of our rooms, we had to circumnavigate their territory without provoking their anger. But in my dreams that inconvenience was compensated for by the occasional discovery of odd neglected rooms, some of them packed with abandoned treasures—a bright French window, a comfortable leather chair or a nice old oak table. These images changed from dream to dream.

And every episode of this serial dream contained, like a logo, the image of the house as seen from the outside. It was a big two-century-old three-storeyed building, slightly dilapidated, with stucco exterior walls painted dark red with white window sills, a tiled roof, and the walls partly covered with ivy. It stood on the bank of a river—the Thames I assumed—and the imitation of Esau's hirsute body; Jacob gives his father a stew made of 'the kids of the goats' instead of venison (an allusion to the angel's provision of the ram that Abraham sacrificed in place of his son Isaac in the previous generational confrontation); and, eventually, Jacob imitates Esau's accent when his father asks for his identity.

22 This is clearly a sublimated reflection on the Arab–Israeli territorial dispute over the Holy Land.

Zinik (right) in the UK, 1982.

nearby bridge was glimpsed occasionally. It
was, no doubt, a very desirable location in
the centre of town (I was at the time renting
accommodation in a London suburb).
Funnily enough, it couldn't have been my
home for real—my family has never lived
on a riverside. But each visit to that place
in my dreams during my first seven years
in London was like a homecoming.

THE DREAM AS SHADOW

And years had passed and I'd forgotten
about that dream. It came back to life, so to
speak, in March last year in Berlin.

And I first came to Berlin in the millen-
nium year: to find out for BBC World Service
how clearly Berliners remembered the geographical division of the city, how impercepti-
ble had the separation between East and West
become 10 years after the Wall's collapse.[23] I
was hypnotized by Berlin. As a Soviet citizen I
had been envious of East Germans: if they
immigrated to West Germany, they were able

Checkpoint Charlie, the best-known crossing point between East and West Germany during the cold war.

23 This reason for my first ever visit to Berlin is only partially true. I, a married man, was so eager to take on this BBC assignment because it gave me another chance to meet up with a German woman with whom I had fallen deeply in love. She was born in the GDR; I was born in the USSR. As a Soviet schoolboy, I was never free of the thought that Germany was still a forbidden zone of Gothic Nazi horrors. A shadow of this childish fear always lingers at the back of the mind of every Soviet Jew. It was there at the back of my mind, too, despite the knowledge that my lover and her generation were no more complicit in their compatriots' Nazi crimes than I was in Soviet atrocities;

to divest themselves of the Soviet outfit while remaining German, speaking the language they had spoken all their lives. The more I learned that the reunification of Germany's two pasts was not so straightforward—that the former East Germans in the western half of the reunited Berlin felt like smugglers who had brought some forbidden contraband with them to a new shore—the more this doubleness, this duplicity, fascinated me, like a criminal who feels compelled to commit again and again the same type of crime. Last year, having inherited some money after my father's death, I started thinking of buying a studio in Berlin.

And, during my recent trip in search of a suitable property, I stayed in a tiny and gloomy rented apartment in a modern block, opposite an imposing building—of brutal modernist architecture—across the canal (Friedrichsgracht). Ironically, this huge building turned out to be none other than Erich Honecker's administrative

and that she had grown up under the Soviet regime which was imposed on her not without some help from my Soviet compatriots. Perhaps I am writing this story in order to discover, or invent, a past that is common to both of us—in the way that lovers are so fond of doing.

Erich Honecker's administrative quarters across Friedrichsgracht, Berlin.

quarters, while the block of apartments in which I was staying had been used to accommodate his administration's servants— drivers, cleaners, typists. It felt eerie being accidentally transported into someone else's political geography as a temporary resident. (We shouldn't forget that Honecker, too, became an exile at the end of his life.) On the other hand, that is what Berlin is all about: just as in Jerusalem, you take a step, without much thought, into a side street and find yourself entrapped in someone else's history. This misplacement of the personal sense of belonging makes everyone in Berlin a kind of Jew.

And the rented apartment was quite depressing in its miniature sanitized meanness. So, despite the terrible weather, I ventured out to see a place I'd never visited before: Monbijoupark in Mitte, where the monument to Adelbert von Chamisso (1781–1838) is located. Chamisso is the author of another German tale that I have

Zinik in front of Chamisso's statue, Mitte, 2009.

known since childhood—a story about a
man who lost his shadow by selling it to the
devil. Chamisso was a son of French émigrés
who escaped the horrors of the French Revolution and settled in Germany at the end
of the eighteenth century. The declaration
of war between France and Prussia made
Chamisso's situation all the more precarious. His difficulties were compounded by a
decree issued by Napoleon in 1806,

whereby any Frenchman found in foreign
military service was to be executed.
Chamisso was torn between two cultures (he
also changed his name, having been born
Louis Charles Adélaïde de Chamissot):

> I am a Frenchman in Germany and a Ger-
> man in France; a Catholic among the Pro-
> testants, Protestant among the Catholics;
> a philosopher among the religious, a
> mundane among the savants, and a
> pedant to the mundane; a Jacobin among
> the aristocrats, and to the democrats a
> nobleman, a man of the Ancien Regime
> . . . Nowhere am I at home![24]

As a born outsider, Chamisso gravitated
naturally to the orbit of other déclassé pari-
ahs—the Jews. Chamisso's tale *Peter Schlemihl*
('schlemihl' is a Yiddish word for an awkward
clumsy person who doesn't belong anywhere:
a man of no consequence) was written in
1813 in German—not in his native French—
and corrected and polished by his new circle
of friends in the famous Berlin salon held in
the attic of the house of Rahel Levin (who

Frontispiece and title page of the first edition of Peter Schlemihl.

24 Adelbert von Chamisso, *Peter Schlemiel: The Man Who Sold His Shadow* (Peter Wortsman trans. and introd.) (New York: Fromm, 1993), p. 12.

would later marry one of Chamisso's good friends, Karl August Varnhagen). In Chamisso's story, a lonely unassuming man, a voyager in a strange city, is approached by the devil who persuades him to sell his soul in exchange for a bottomless purse. As a result of the deal, the man loses his bride and, shunned by the rest of humanity, goes into exile, seeking refuge in distant uninhabited lands. Although the initial motive of the protagonist's action is money, for Chamisso, who wrote the story, it was a straightforward fable about the lost identity of an émigré—a bilingual exile who has lost his sense of belonging. People without shadows are, of course, those without a past. Or as Arthur Koestler says in his book, *Thieves in the Night* (1946): 'A country is a shadow which a nation throws, and for two thousand years we were a nation without a shadow.'[25]

And my way to the Chamisso monument, located in the old Jewish quarter of Berlin, lay along the part of the river

25 At the end of the story, Peter Schlemihl becomes a traveller and ethnographer, a sort of globe-trotting naturalist,
transporting himself across distant lands in a pair of Seven
League Boots as if in a private jet. This ending provides a
remarkable example of life imitating art. It was a prophetic
insight by the hero of the book into the author's fate. In
1812, Chamisso enrolled in the Faculty of Medicine at the
University of Berlin. He began to study botany, zoology,
geology, anatomy, physiology, and comparative anatomy.
He later wrote that the University of Berlin 'was, is and will
remain my fatherland'. When the war resumed yet again
in 1815 after Napoleon's return from Elba, Chamisso
sought and was granted the opportunity to escape the
problems of his personal life. A few years after his book's
publication, Chamisso became a traveller himself, joining
a team of scientists aboard the Russian ship *Rurik* on a
round-the-world trip. None other than Charles Darwin
called him a 'justly distinguished naturalist'. But Chamisso
did not believe in the evolution of species. Though he was
primarily a botanist, his most significant contribution to
science is generally judged to be his zoological paper on
the jellyfish 'salpa'. In his paper, Chamisso describes for
the first time the phenomenon of the alternation of
generations: the salpa (a tunicate) alternates its form of
existence from generation to generation. In one generation it is an individual, free-swimming form; in the next,
it becomes a colonial form in which individuals join together to form a larger organism. At the time of the birth
of nationalism in Europe, Chamisso's discovery provided

Spree, with its locks and rail bridges, which is still used by rusty old barges overloaded with goods. The further you progress towards Monbijoubrücke, with Museum Island to your right, the stronger the contrast becomes between the imperial architecture on the right-hand side and the semi-industrial landscape with warehouses, garages and shut-down factories on the left—the remains and ruins of East Berlin's neglected past. The stormy weather blurred the contours of the buildings around, so that columns and arches could be confused with the cranes and winches on the barges, while museum buildings under scaffolding looked like the carcasses of sailing ships. The raging rain swallowed the borders between sky and earth and hit pedestrians from unexpected directions with squalls of wind as if from a riot policeman's water cannon. I couldn't feel the ground under my feet, as if I was suspended in a heavy cloud of water drops.

an amazing metaphor, borrowed from Nature, for the changes that nations of the world undergo throughout history—alternating between liberal individualism and collective conformity. So original was this view that it took many years for it to be accepted, it being regarded by some as just another fabulous invention by the author of *Peter Schlemihl* (see Edward Mornin, *Through Alien Eyes: The Visit of the Russian Ship Rank to San Francisco in 1816 and the Men behind the Visit*, Oxford and New York: Peter Lang, 2002).

That's how Peter Schlemihl must have felt
crossing continents in his magic Seven
League Boots. I experienced a similar
feeling once on a little boat that takes
tourists as close as possible to the gigantic
splash of the Niagara Falls.

And when I reached the Monbijoubrücke, the rain suddenly stopped. To
my right was the massive squatting dome
of the Bode Collection, oppressive in its
semi-Byzantine decorum, housing antiqui-
ties of the ancient world. There was something Soviet about this museum building,
shrouded in a didactic aura of knowledge
and tradition. I suddenly felt a slight shift
in my perception of time and space, as if
I'd lost my sense of location, not only
geographically but historically too, which
often happens in cities whose past is overcrowded with competing historical forces.
But the heavy rain clouds that were hanging
in the sky like wet washing on the line broke
up and ran astray.

And the light was divided from the
darkness. Suddenly the sun shone everywhere.

And I looked to the left and was in-
stantly frozen by the shock of recognition.
On the banks of the river stood the exact
replica of the house that I had seen in
my dreams 20 years ago. A slightly dilapidated building, with a tiled roof and stucco
walls, painted dark red, partly covered
with ivy. How did it get there? The dream
I once had was a shadow—a mirror image
reflected in my mind—of the house that
now stood in front of my eyes. Its shadow
was long enough to reach me first, before
the real thing. It felt like this dream image
had been lifted from my mind, reproduced
in brick and mortar as if on a Hollywood
set, and placed on the banks of the river
Spree. And I said to my companion (I was
not alone on this walk): 'I know this house.'

And we went through the gates and
into the yard and approached the main

porch at the back of the building. Strangely enough, it looked like the entrance to an official institution. '*Humboldt Universität zu Berlin*', read the plaque next to the doorway, and with my rudimentary German I deciphered that it housed the Department of Blood Transfusions and Immunology. I stood there, totally baffled. Besides the symbolic link with the notion of blood—everyone's family past—this building's function had nothing to with the warm sentimental feelings I associated with the house of my London dreams that it outwardly resembled. The building was clearly just a part of Humboldt University's medical faculty. Perhaps, it was the same medical school where Cham- isso had studied. But what did it have to do with the family house of my dreams?

THE GRANDPARENTS' LARDER

And, as it turned out, it had a lot to do with it. In one of the episodes of my serial dream, I happen to enter a room I have

The dream house on the banks of the Spree, Berlin, 2008.

Charité

UNIVERSITÄTSKLINIKUM · MEDIZINISCHE FAKULTÄT
DER HUMBOLDT-UNIVERSITÄT ZU BERLIN
CAMPUS CHARITÉ MITTE

**INSTITUT FÜR
TRANSFUSIONSMEDIZIN**

The plaque next to the doorway to the dream house by the Spree.

never been in before. Most of the *lebensraum*
is occupied by a huge bed with a carved
headboard. In it, propped up by many a
pillow, lies my grandmother: she is feeling
unwell and remains in bed, but is immaculately dressed, her hair carefully coiffured;
she is reading—there is a book in her
hands. The rest of the wall behind the bed
is covered in bookshelves from the floor to
ceiling, packed with precious old volumes *in
folio*, bound in leather. 'Why have I never
used this beautiful library?', I ask myself. I
pick up one of the tomes from the shelves
and start leafing through it. To my great
disappointment, I discover that not only
this but all the volumes in the home library
are in Latin, and all of them are on the subject of medicine. They are of no use to me.
They are medical books. They belonged to
my grandfather, a family doctor.

And, throughout my childhood, I felt
more at home with my grandparents than
with my mother and father. As long as I

can remember, my parents would quarrel
every day, even physically attacking each
other in my presence. In the heat of a row
they would put me in front of them and
ask: who would I choose to stay with if they
divorced? (Ever since, I've hated making
choices.) Or else, they would try to rid
themselves of my presence in the dreary
communal apartment at any given opportunity, as was the habit of the most Soviet
parents in the harsh reality of post-war Russia. Before I was old enough to be sent to
pioneer camps and to other state funded
institutions such as the all-day local school,
I had spent most of my earlier childhood
with my grandparents.

And my grandfather—my mother's father—was a local doctor in the small township of Bobrik-Donskoy, in a mining region
about 100 kilometres from Moscow. The little hamlet where they had their house was
set in the picturesque countryside. The years
after the war were not the most prosperous

in the history of Russia. So, local peasants would pay their doctor by barter for medical services. They would bring eggs and dairy produce, game and meat cuts, seasonal fruit and vegetables. Every corner of the big—or what I remembered as big—house was packed with this agricultural bribery.

And the smell of fresh apples, laid out everywhere in the house and left to ripen on the shelves and even under the beds, was overwhelming. In the storage room next to the kitchen stood a row of wooden barrels, each with a different type of pickle: cucumbers in salt and brine, marinated red and green tomatoes, cabbage pickled with carrots, and most importantly, a barrel with pickled apples.[26] The household was run smoothly by Grandma and her 'helping hands' recruited from among the locals—a charwoman and a cook—whom no one would call 'servants'. The most memorable thing for me was breakfast, with its steady

26 These apples return us to the motif of innocence in the Garden of Eden. But since the apples in this instance are pickled, we are speaking here of a Russian way of treating temptation: just pickle it!

Adam and Eve *by Lucas Cranach the Elder (1472–1553)*.

Zinik in Bobrik-Donskoy, c.1950.

ritual of eating a boiled egg—and hot
bagels with jam and tea—as I had been
taught by my grandfather, cutting the top of
the egg off rather than smashing it with a

spoon, as everyone else did in Russia. This procedure was supervised by Grandpa himself at the head of the table, always clean-shaven and immaculately dressed in a white shirt with cufflinks and a waistcoat, ready to put on his black jacket to go to the clinic. Each time I felt distraught at having odd bits of crumbled eggshell in my mouth in my spoonful of egg, Grandpa would calm me down by saying that eggshell contains calcium that was good for my bones which were, in his medical opinion, too weak. (His diagnostics proved perfectly right, as my later scoliosis has shown, resembling Dwarf Long Nose's crooked spine.) In short, the most minute aspects of my daily routine were taken care of by my grandparents, only enhancing my sensation of this house as being Paradise.

And I experienced fear in this household only once. One day, left to my own devices, I was wandering around the house, playing hide-and-seek with myself and opening the doors of the wall cupboards at random. Inside one of them, next to the kitchen, the body of a skinned hare[27] hung from a large hook, rotting slightly as game should before being cooked: its bloody skinless flesh, complete with the mutilated head, looked like the pilloried victim of some horrible execution. This was the only incident, as far as I can remember, which seriously stained, in my mind, the otherwise immaculately bright picture of sheer bliss.

And the question is: was the house that I dreamed about in London inspired by this image of my grandfather's house? Ostensibly, the dream house looked totally different. It had the foreign look of a solid big town house in one of the European capitals. My grandparents, in contrast to that dream, lived in a cheap mid-terrace house, the front of which was plastered dusty yellow and grey, with a tin and tarpaulin roof and no ivy. There was no river nearby either, apart from a pathetic brook, which was used

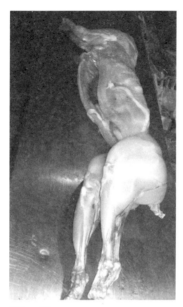

Skinned hare.

27 Skinning is the ultimate punishment: it deprives the victim of any trace of identity. The creature is not only dead—it is nobody. (The Greek god Apollo was fond of skinning his competitors in the arts, for instance Marsyas.) That's what Esau most probably wanted to do to Jacob: skin him. This total nakedness is also crucial in the treatment of prisoners or army recruits. You must remove all your clothes before you are given a new uniform. Naked, the person is like a mannequin, ready to be dressed up in accordance with someone else's design—your new uniform as a sewage duct, overgrown with elderberry and wolfberry bushes, nettles and cowslips. In short, the house I had dreamed about was clearly an idealized fictional past that I had constructed in my mind; but, perhaps, it was a fanciful projection of the real place—a radically improved past—of my grandparents' home, where I had spent, for real, so many happy days, and where love and care ruled supreme. Or so I believed.[28]

ACROSS THE RIVER INTO THE PAST

And at this point I decided to look into the family papers. I did it reluctantly; because dealing with old documents always makes me feel, paradoxically, even more desolate, rootless, less linked to my present: a past disturbs the present with unexpected links to something which is very difficult to identify with your life as you used to know it. Look at that photo of me as a five-year-old child watching my grandfather shaving himself [p. 75]. How could I recognize in

of life tailored for you. In the tale of Dwarf Long Nose, the witch, in order to turn little Jacob into a squirrel, first takes off his clothes and then puts on the squirrel fur.

Zinik's grandfather, shaving, c.1950.

28 The little hamlet in which my grandparents' house stood was not as idyllic as it had once seemed to me. I now recollect a scene which, as a boy, I would see out of my window with repetitive regularity: a local lad, totally

this blonde little boy with a turned-up nose myself as I am now—with my grizzly grey hair, my flabby wrinkled face and protruding Jewish proboscis? Was it really me?[29]

And as I look now at the little boy in the faded old photo, I notice that he is staring not at his Grandpa, a gentleman having his morning shave, but at his old-fashioned razor blade. Is the boy scared of this long sharp instrument? Does he connect it with the horrifying image of the naked flesh hanging from the hook in the cupboard under the stairs? Is he trembling at the thought that his fate might be similar to that of a skinned hare?[30] All these are questions for psychoanalysts to answer. But if you follow the boy's gaze in the photo closely, you will realize that he is fascinated, even hypnotized, not by the razor but by the way the old man is wiping the foam from the blade. He is using brown wrapping paper to do so—we see heaps of it in drunk, would become unhinged and chase his mother around the courtyard with an axe in his hand, shouting, 'I will kill you.' She would try to run away from him as fast as possible, circling the yard without abandoning him altogether, and shout back, 'Mind the blade, sonny, don't cut your hands, sweetheart!' This, for me, was the first encounter with unconditional love.

29 Perhaps we shouldn't connect these two bodies at all—me as the boy and me as the ageing man. Perhaps they are linked, but not through degradation of the flesh or transmogrification of personality traits. Siamese twins are linked in both space and time, and yet they remain totally separate individuals. We—our younger and older selves—may have a common ancestor and a shared body but we are not directly connected with one another. I am similarly at a loss when someone is trying to establish a link between me and the Russia of Ivan the Terrible or the Israel of King David.

30 At that time I didn't know the biblical story of the Binding of Isaac, Abraham's attempt at sacrificing Isaac to God. Was it pre-installed in the hard disk of my ancestral memory? Had the skinned hare, a surrogate of the holy lamb that had prevented human sacrifice, triggered this memory? In any case, I should not have been scared of my grandfather; grandfathers are always in cahoots with grandchildren against fathers as the story of Isaac, his father Abraham and grandfather God shows.

front of him on the table. I don't know why
he didn't use an ordinary towel, a napkin or
a piece of old cloth instead—like barbers
used to? Was it the post-war era of auster-
ity? Or, had he received an unexpected sur-
plus of wrapping paper that came, perhaps,
from local hospital deliveries and was not to
be wasted? Of this whole scene I still remember most vividly and sharply the physical sound of the blade being pressed and
moved in between the folds of the harsh
matt brown wrapping paper. I am still aller-
gic to that sound and shudder slightly at
the memory of it.[31]

And it was in envelopes made of this
brown paper that some of the documents
from my family archive were kept: old pho-
tographs, some letters, notes and certificates, records of employment, drafts of
wills and even an unfinished poem by my
grandmother. The most important find
were two diplomas on crumbling velum

31 The use of such brown paper was always associated in my mind with the officialdom of state bureaucracy. You notice this paper and you are transported into suffocating, badly lit and badly painted corridors of some state institution or other in which an unwashed human crowd is queuing up for an uncertain answer to an unasked question. Bad news comes through your letterbox in those very envelopes, even in England, even now. This brown paper is an international emblem of unhappiness.

foolscap paper. In Gothic lettering the documents ceremoniously announced that Mendel Glaezerow had studied medicine at the 'Universitat zu Konigsberg' from 1908 until 1911 and then graduated as a Doctor of Medicine in 1913 at the 'Friedrich-Wilhelms Universitat zu Berlin'. It clicked—Berlin! *Die ganze Welt* was not to be conquered yet but at least I had made the first step on the path to Berlin. It was a great disappointment, though, that the university at which my grandfather had studied was not Humboldt University, to which the building I had recognized in Berlin belonged.

And as a last ditch attempt I turned to the biggest depot of ancestral memory: Google. I googled 'Friedrich-Wilhelms Universitat' and came up with the revelation that it was none other than the former name of what has been known since 1949 as Humboldt University. The medical school

Mendel Glaezerow's diploma.

of that university was located at the same place in Berlin in my grandfather's time as it is now: off Monbijoubrücke, on river Spree. The title of his doctoral dissertation was *Über den zeitlichen Verlauf der Harnsäurebildung bei der Durchblutung der Gänseleber* ('The temporal stages of the formation of uric acid during the blood circulation in goose liver'). That is, he was indeed involved in blood research—the subject studied at the medical school near Monbijoubrücke, as was stated on the plaque at the entrance.[32]

And there could be quite a few mystical links connecting the image of the house in my dreams with the real building in Berlin. One may share a Wittgensteinian belief that everything which the human mind can possibly conceive will eventually be materialized; or a Platonic concept of dreams as ideas being the prime movers behind material objects' existence—that is, the real

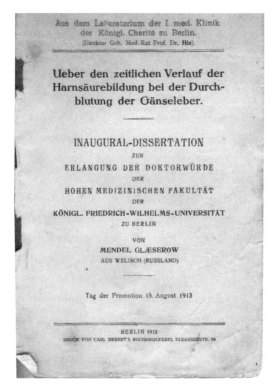

The title page of Glaezerow's dissertation.

32 I should also note that goose liver pate was a staple delicacy in my grandparents' household.

world is a mere shadow of the dream. Or, in reverse fashion, a real object in the past might, under certain circumstances and weather conditions, resurface as a ghost or a dream in the mind of a particularly sensitive person, thus inducing a link with his past. The most fanciful hypothesis would be to suggest that every Jew has access to a common ancestral reservoir of memory—a collective consciousness (Google was developed by a Russian Jew)—so that a grandson would be able to remember the things his grandfather had experienced. (If true, this would serve as powerful pro-Zionist proof of the existence of links between modern Jews and the land of the Bible.)

And there is also a rational explanation to this, though it's no less difficult to prove. There might have been a photograph of this Berlin medical school on Grandpa's desk or in a family photo album. (Chamisso called the University of Berlin his 'Fatherland'.) I must have seen it and had it imprinted on my brain's convolutions. Many years later it was reactivated in the form of an ideal family past—a house in my dreams, my 'private Zion'. Whatever the explanation, the fact is that a made-up past, fictionalized from my dreams, turned out to be rooted in a firm reality. More than that, this reality was loaded with the political history of the time, which would affect my own future.

BEYOND THE PALE

And Mendel Glaezerow must have been proud of his medical education, first as a pharmacist and eventually as a doctor. Not only had this profession liberated him from all the restrictions and quotas imposed on a Jew wishing to move beyond the pale of settlement, it had also allowed him to marry my grandmother. According to family legend, my grandmother's father, Abram Ginsburg, from the prosperous town of

Mogilyov, was one of the richest men of Belarus, which was then a part of the Russian empire.[33] He was a timber merchant[34] and rented a huge Russian estate in the area, which he ran with pomp and panache: a four-horse carriage was always at his disposal and dinner parties and charity balls were held regularly for the local gentry in the huge house. He must have looked down on his daughter's choice of Mendel Glaezerow, one of five brothers from what had been

A street in modern-day Velizh.

33 Where did all the millions of Jews in Eastern Europe come from? Most European Jews do not know their ancestors beyond their great-grandfathers' generation. The suggestion that they were the descendants of those dispersed from the land of Israel by ancient Romans cannot be supported by any data on European Jewish population. The most convincing hypothesis is that of Arthur Koestler: Judaic tribes had spread over Europe from the mighty Khazar kingdom—that occupied a vast territory between the Black Sea and the Caspian Sea—of a Turkic people who adopted Judaism as their state religion. (Linguists believe that 'yarmulke' is a Turkic word.) No less fascinating is the suggestion by Alexander Melamid (co-founder of the Rubber Band Society of the US and of the Safety Pin Society of the UK) that all of today's European Jews are descendants of a Protestant sect from the Middle Ages who fancied themselves as biblical Jews. Such a sect must have been persecuted; members of the commune must have been forced to stick together and marry each other. (The Subbotniks are a good example.) As a result of several centuries of such isolation, a distinct physical—'Jewish'—type was developed, which differed, of course, from country to country, reflecting the geography and the race in which the sect sprang up. But a common resemblance also emerged, because one's profession (that of a school teacher, a stamp collector or a diamond polisher) ultimately left a mark on one's appearance.

34 Wood was the hottest commodity at the time of the booming railway industry.

a family of carpenters for many generations in the little township of Velizh.[35] Although one of my grandfather's brothers had done the woodcarving for one of the tsar's palaces, as a boy, Mendel—as his short autobiography tells us—had to do manual work to save up for schooling in order to become a pharmacist's assistant. So, Mendel asking for the hand of Ginsburg's beloved daughter, Blyuma, was met with initial refusal. It was only the fear of dispossession in the face of the first Russian revolution in February 1905 and the abdication of the tsar that made Ginsburg accept a marriage proposal from a carpenter's son. It looks as if it was my grandmother's dowry that enabled Mendel to go first to Konigsberg,[36] and then to Berlin, to study. Blyuma (whose official Russian name was 'Lyubov', which means 'love'), a graduate of the first women's gymnasium in St Petersburg, was herself a dentist with a degree. It was her money that paid for my grandfather's stay in Berlin. But

35 It was in Velizh that, in 1823, the first trial for ritual murder took place in Russia. A local Jewish family—whose name was, incidentally, Berlin—was accused of killing a Christian child and draining his blood to be used in the celebration of Passover. After 10 years of investigation and imprisonment, all the accused were acquitted and those witnesses who had fabricated their evidence were exiled to Siberia. This case inspired Mikhail Lermontov's poem, 'The Spaniards' (1830).

Zinik with his father, Efim Gluzberg, in Moscow, 1988.

36 Mendel's son-in-law (my father) lost his leg during the Second World War on the way to Konigsberg, which was levelled to the ground by the Soviet army (not without a little help from the Royal Air Force). Severely wounded, my

pregnant with their first child, she went back
to Moscow, where, as doctors with diplomas,
they were now allowed to settle down.

And this is not the occasion to tell the
full story of my grandfather's peregrina-
tions. Mendel's letters from Berlin to
Moscow reveal the character of a dexterous,
ambitious and hard-working young man,
trying to live up to the expectations of his
rich and beautiful young wife; a student
with modest means but with a huge ap-
petite for the social and artistic life of the
German capital. Back in Russia a year later,
his German doctorate in medicine was con-
firmed by the University of Moscow.
According to his brief autobiography,
during the First World War, he was sent to
the front line as a staff doctor in a military
hospital. He took part in the Bolshevik
Revolution as a doctor in the little Ukrain-
ian town of Shpola, where he was later
arrested as a Red Army collaborator and

father was demobilized and was sent back to his parents' home in Moscow for convalescence. If he hadn't been injured on the front line, he would have come back after the war to his first wife whom he had left behind in Siberia. He wouldn't have met my mother in Moscow. And I wouldn't have been born. But whose shell had hit him, after all, that caused the loss of his limb? The shell came from the Nazis, of course. Therefore, I should hold the Nazis responsible for my birth.

Mendel Glaezerow, c.1930.

threatened with execution by a White
Army officer; he worked in Uzbekistan,
where he was active in building a brave new
and healthy Soviet society; he was evacu-
ated to the land beyond the Urals before
settling down, following the Second World
War, in Bobrik-Donskoy, where he took
care to teach me how to eat a soft-boiled
egg. Two-and-a-half pages of his autobiography were clearly written for the Soviet

A page from Glaezerow's autobiography.

authorities to show his revolutionary credentials in 1949, the horrific year of the renewed wave of Stalinist paranoia about foreign spies and of the fight against so-called cosmopolitanism.[37] The autobiography ends with the obligatory Soviet pledge: 'I have never been a member of any anti-Soviet organization, never been under criminal investigation or imprisoned by the Soviet authorities, and have no relatives abroad.' It was my turn, a quarter century later, to falsify my past in search of nonexistent relatives abroad.

And it was very difficult to say now to what extent Mendel had falsified his past as a proletarian revolutionary. He had always been away on some business assignment. And then, there was an enigmatic period in the 1930s when he hadn't lived at home for many years. In the little book that records the places of his employment year by year, there is a blank space for most of the 1930s. My mother once told me—when I was searching for a relative abroad to support my exit visa application—that there was a period when Grandpa lived abroad permanently. With regular intervals, once every

In front of the Moscow apartment, 1952.

37 I was four years old at the time, but very alert and vigilant for a child. One day, standing by the gate of our courtyard, I saw a man come out from our building and walk off suspiciously fast. A future 'Pioneer' and 'Young Communist', I might have been busy with an ice cream but, in fact, I was already on his trail. Evidently, the suspicious man guessed somebody was onto him. He crossed the few months, a black limousine would pull up unexpectedly at our apartment block. Grandpa would appear in his three-piece suit, spend an hour or so with the family, drink tea, kiss his beloved children and be driven away again to an unknown destination.

And now I know what this destination was. His brief autobiography states it clearly: from 1931 to 1938 he was employed by the People's Commissariat for Internal Affairs (NKVD, later the KGB). It transpires that he was told to open a clinic in Kovno (now Kaunas) in Lithuania. He had to file regular reports on the changing mood of the local population in that divided country, torn between conflicting and aggressive claims on its territory by Russia, Germany and Poland, which was, at that time, occupying parts of Lithuania, including Vilnius. Kaunas, therefore, assumed the status of the national capital in which pro-Russian tendencies in politics had to be taken seriously.[38]

road. I was sharp. I turned the corner too. He glanced over his shoulder and turned another corner. I followed suit. Now I was certain. He was a spy. He was an experienced spy, because hardly had I turned the corner when I saw him make a break across the street. I followed. When my spy dashed into the baker's, I just didn't know what to do. There was real crush in the baker's. I couldn't pick my spy out in the crowd. The baker's was about to close and presently I was shoved outside. I stood by the doorway—looked left and right. I'd strayed on to a street I'd never been in before. I was lost. I knew I'd never be able to find my way home. I started to howl, hot tears streaming down my cheeks. Then suddenly a grown-up face loomed over me. To my horror, I saw it was the spy. 'What are you crying for, sonny?' the spy asked in honeyed tones. 'But I know you, don't I, sonny? You live on stairway no. 4. I'm the new house manager. So, we're lost, aren't we?' He took my hand and dragged me home. As it happens, a year later, they did arrest him as an enemy of the people.

38 It was Claudia Sinnig, an author and a distinguished German translator of Lithuanian literature, who opened for me the book of Central European history in general. It happened when we had both been visiting Vilnius. I was following my father's one-legged steps on the way to Kaliningrad (former Konigsberg) and Vilnius—the 'Jerusalem of Lithuania'—is the usual transit stop. Like everyone who was born in Moscow and grew up in the USSR, I was ignorant of the world beyond the limits of my

My grandfather, therefore, was laying down the foundation for the building of the future Soviet Empire. He was creating a future for me, from which I, 40 years later, succeeded in escaping.[39]

TROPHIES OF THE COMMUNAL PAST

And what and whom was Mendel Glaezerow trying to avoid when he moved around from one end of the Russian empire to another, from one exotic employment to the next, from Uzbekistan to Kaunas?[40] A possible answer is provided by the note my grandmother wrote before she died. There, on a ruled page torn out of a school exercise book, she listed in her shaky handwriting all that her children had to know about her funeral arrangements, including a detailed description of how she should be dressed for the occasion: how to do her hair, which fabric for the frock and what kind of underwear to choose—she even insisted that the colour immediate Russian preoccupations; I was totally oblivious to the complexity of life in the countries under Soviet occupation, such as Lithuania, which, to Soviet citizens, was no more than a provincial resort. Little did I know that my personal history was greatly entangled with it.

39 One man's dream is another's hard labour. Stalinists would fabricate fictitious historical causes to justify the miserable Soviet present. In order to compensate for the present emotional vacuum, we reinvent our past. But it is not ours. It is borrowed from somebody else's myths or tradition—the Bible or the Scandinavian sagas, the French Enlightenment or Prussian militarism. This past, adopted and adapted to suit our aspirations and temperament, is then imposed on others—on our neighbours, sometimes in their own territories. We create past events that are provoked by our present ideological causes, as George Eliot expressed in her novel, *Daniel Deronda* (1876). This rediscovered (or manufactured) past, in turn, provokes our neighbours to rethink their own past, which they were unaware of before. This is what happened to the Palestinians, who discovered their own national identity after it was awoken in them by the Zionist myth. My friend Meir Wieseltier, the most clear-minded of Israeli poets, epitomized this idea in his poem 'Passengers':

> When the bus arrived in Tel-Aviv, I was struck
>   by their sleep:
> two men, thirtyish, dark skinned, dressed up
>   in new

trousers, shirts, ties, everything gleaming
under their two well-cut blank profiles,
close to each other, a sculpted closeness,
their features unmistakably Hittite.
Then I knew that their whole festive rig
had grown on them without their realising.
Sleepers for ninety generations, swept into
    the city at a gallop,
and opening their eyes now, amazed and
    briefly emboldened,
were about to crash unbridled into the dust of
    our lives.
And I knew we were braking, pulling into the
    Central Bus Station
where something horrendous would befall them.

[From Meir Wieseltier, *Something Optimistic, the Making of Poems* (Shirley Kaufman trans.) (Tel-Aviv: Siman Keriah, 1976)].

40 If we zoom in on the history of my grandfather's birthplace, Velizh, we can see how the complicated routes of his life can be traced to the history of this little town near Vitebsk. In mediaeval times, it was a border fortress of the grand duchy of Lithuania, captured, abandoned and recaptured by the Russians with persistent regularity. My grandfather's less-than-expected stay in Uzbekistan is linked, perhaps, to the fact that his contemporary—and possible friend—Max Penson (1893–1959), a celebrated

Soviet photographer, was also born in Velizh. Penson participated in the World Exhibition in Paris (1937), winning the Grand Prix Award for Uzbek Madonna, a portrait of a young Uzbek woman, nursing her child in public. He also photographed the construction of the Grand Fergana Canal. Penson, alongside Alexander Rodchenko and Sergei Eisenstein, had contributed to the creation of the mythological USSR of my happy childhood as a religion of the radiant future. But the campaign against formalism in the arts and anti-Western paranoia that gripped the country after the Second World War made him an outcast and, in the 1950s, he died a broken man. General Rodzianko, who negotiated the fate of the Denikin White Army in Ukraine (where my grandfather was sentenced to death, but was eventually saved) with the British government, was also born in Velizh. The most famous native of Velizh is Nikolai Przhevalsky, an ethnographer whose name is associated with the breed of horses he discovered in Mongolia. I could never understand why this particular scientist and his horse were studied so thoroughly in Soviet schools until I saw a photo of him: he is the spitting image of Stalin; or, rather, the reverse is true: Stalin is the spitting image of him. It is a well-known fact that, while staying in Tbilisi, Przhevalsky employed Stalin's mother as a charwoman. Nine months later, Stalin was born.

of her shoes should match that of the coffin. A lot was left to her children's imagination —for example, the choice of the cemetery. The list of instructions, though, ends with a firm plea: 'Under no condition am I to be buried in the same grave as my husband.'

And when, a few months ago, I came across this note, the bright picture of my ideal childhood in my grandparents' house suddenly darkened. The prelapsarian abundance of pickled cucumbers and unconditional love was lost for me forever. In the same bunch of documents, I discovered a short poem that my grandmother wrote on my grandfather's return from Berlin: 'I've been pining away, waiting for you, but instead of amorous rapture, I drank a cup of poison!' There was, clearly, another woman in Berlin.[41] The complicated course of Mendel's life could be explained by the numerous love affairs he had had in different parts of the world. Bobrik-

Zinik (left) with Grandma and half-sister, c.1950.

Zinik (far right) with Grandma, an uncle and a cousin, c.1950.

41 See note 23, p. 51.

Grandma's poem.

Donskoy was the last stop. Then, on a miserable state pension, ageing and ailing, he had had no choice but to move back to Moscow. This old-fashioned gentleman with impeccable manners, this globetrotter and

Zinik (right) with Grandpa and a cousin, c.1950.

immaculately dressed doctor was to die in a
crummy old Soviet apartment which he had
once owned but was now forced to share
with his hapless children and their rapidly
growing families.

And, despite their mutual hatred of over 40 years, my grandparents had to share the same bed—space was scarce. I was born in a room of 12 square metres that I shared with my parents and my stepsister.[42] But when Grandpa was dying, he wouldn't allow his wife, my beautiful grandmother Blyuma, to touch his ailing body. In the last stages of his illness, he suffered terrible pains—he was seemingly dying of cancer of the bladder—and I remember his shrieks of agony. It was not his wife, my grandmother, but his daughter who helped him when he needed to use the urine bottle.[43]

And he was the first human being whom I saw laid in a coffin. The dead man in the box was as frighteningly immobile as the skinned hare in the cupboard.

And now I can vividly recollect the room in our apartment which my uncle's family occupied and in which Grandpa's last days were spent. I visualize, behind the glass doors of the sideboard and on top of the

A typical communal kitchen in Moscow, c. 1960.

42 My father used to seek asylum from that overcrowded madness in his parents' room in another communal apartment located on the same landing. His desk was there and he used the space in his parents' room as his study. When my aunt, my father's sister, returned from Moscow with her demobilized husband and settled down in Grandpa's room, the desk was taken away, stripping my father of his

upright piano, an amazing collection, exhibited as if in an antique shop, of porcelain
figurines of animals and fairies, and vases
and dishes painted over with magical images. In the centre of this heap of treasures

Porcelain clock in Zinik's uncle's room.

stood a huge clock made of porcelain, with
angels and cupids guarding its face with
chimes. Each time a guest at the house
would marvel at this miracle in the midst
of grim Stalinist Moscow, my uncle would
explain with an assumed indifference and a

workplace. My parents were outraged that no one had thought of consulting them about it: bastards, traitors, enemies of the people! The case went to court and my father won. But the right to residence had to be validated by spending the night there for at least once a week. Even though I was still in nursery, I was sent to the enemy camp for the weekly nightshift. I was put on a foldaway bed and, in the darkness, I would listen to my relatives' conversations. They would say terrible things about Mummy and Daddy but I had to keep quiet and pretend that I was asleep. They knew that I wasn't, and would keep saying more and more hurtful things. I would plug my ears and dig my head under the pillow. Nothing helped. And, to this day, nothing helps. That was my first banishment from heaven—my first emigration.

43 The urine bottle is called 'utka' in Russian—which means a duck—because of the duck-like shape of the bottle. Recall here that the circulation of blood in the duck (or goose) liver was the subject of my grandfather's doctoral dissertation written in Berlin. The magic herb *niesmitlust* ('sneezewithease' in English) that turns Jacob from the ugly dwarf back into a beautiful boy could not have been found without the help of an enchanted goose (who was, in fact, a beautiful maiden turned into the goose by the same evil witch who had cast the spell on Jacob). My grandfather's patronymic was Jacob.

wave of the hand that masked his pride at
his achievements: 'Those are the trophies.'
These *tropheinoye dobro* (captured goodies)
were, of course, items of the officially sanc-
tioned looting, distributed between high
ranking officers, such as my uncle, to be
brought back to Russia from Germany. I
wonder what my grandfather felt while
looking at those relics of his adopted German past, of his Berlin years, now exhibited
as the spoils of war.

THE ACT OF RECOGNITION

And yet, all these facts that have exposed
the illusory aspects of my childhood cannot
destroy the unshakeable sensation of bliss
that I feel each time I think of the years I
spent in my grandparents' house. There
exists in our heads the obstinate reality of
a dream which is impossible to eradicate
from memory and which we are reluctant to
denounce as an illusion. Should I discount
this 'elevating deception', in Alexander

Pushkin's words, as a delusion, discard it as pure fiction? What if the building that I discovered on my walks around Berlin, where my grandfather had studied medicine, didn't exactly resemble the house I had dreamed of after all? Even if I insisted that it did, who would be able to prove their identical appearance? And how could I be certain that this resemblance was not a fanciful delusion—a desire to link my Soviet past to my present—associated with Berlin?[44]

And my answer is: all these provocative questions about the semblance, resemblance or dissemblance with regard to the link between my dream house and the one I saw in Berlin are irrelevant. We are obsessed with checking the veracity of facts and the identity of the objects we deal with. But I exist—with my dreams and my guts —regardless of what others think of me, regardless of what identity card is put into my breast pocket. My experience has taught me that we can achieve truth not just by discarding false facts and exposing fake identities. The act of recognition is a quicker and more reliable guide to the truth: we momentarily recognize a familiar face in a crowded room and find our way home by recognizing familiar corners. Something clicked in my mind when I saw a house on the banks of river Spree. Unexpectedly, in it I recognized the house that I was already familiar with—God knows how. And that house turned out to be the medical school that my grandfather graduated from. I recognized something in a foreign reality—in the solid history of another nation—something that was directly linked to my family's past.[45]

And every act of recognition conceals both the desire and the fear of being recognized.

And it was this recognition that was the miracle. The rest was storytelling.

44 The suspicion of deception is infectious. It also leads to violence: when people become doubtful of your past they begin to question the legitimacy of your present wellbeing, as it happens in our private life and, eventually, in the life of nations.

45 Isaac recognizes the first-born son in Jacob despite striking evidence to the contrary: 'The voice is Jacob's voice, but the hands are the hands of Esau' [Genesis 27:22]. True recognition is as different from an illusion (or delusion) of familiarity as faith is different from obsession.

The present book had its genesis in a speech delivered by the author at the Eurozine 22nd European Meeting of Cultural Journals, Vilnius, 8–11 May 2009, and published at www.eurozine.com.

INDEX
ON CENSORSHIP

Index on Censorship is Britain's leading organization promoting freedom of expression. Our award-winning magazine and website provide a window for original, challenging and intelligent writing on this vital issue around the world. Our international projects in media, arts and education put our philosophy into action.

For information and enquiries go to
www.indexoncensorship.org,
or email enquiries@indexoncensorship.org

www.indexoncensorship.org

THE IMPACT OF THE FRENCH REVOLUTION

The French Revolution embodied, in ....ations, the emergence of the modern politi.... ..e possible a new understanding of class politics, secular... ... and revolutionary transformation which inspired, argues Iain Hampsher-Monk, the whole worldwide communist experiment of the twentieth century. In this authoritative anthology of key political texts exploring the impact of this period on the British experience, Hampsher-Monk examines the variety, influence and profundity of major thinkers such as Burke, Wollstonecraft, Paine and Godwin, along with the impact of other, less celebrated contemporary writers.

This anthology is intended for tutors and students (at all levels from first-year undergraduate upwards) wishing to study the political theories generated in Britain by the Revolution: not only ideals such as liberty but more pervasive political principles such as secularism and individualism that emerged during this turbulent period. The writings anthologised here are excerpted in such a way as to maintain the coherence and line of thought throughout each work, and thus students are shown whole arguments, and not merely isolated 'ideas'. *The Impact of the French Revolution* will be an important resource in its own right, and a major teaching tool for courses on the revolutionary period, the history of ideas, and political thought.

IAIN HAMPSHER-MONK is Professor of Political Theory at the University of Exeter. A founder-editor of the journal *History of Political Thought*, his many publications include the prize-winning study, *A History of Modern Political Thought* (1994). He is preparing an edition of Burke's *Reflections* for the series of Cambridge Texts in the History of Political Thought.